Max Hodes describes himself as nobody in particular. In fact, he's an Edinburgh-born journalist who writes an often funny column called 'Chatalong With Max' in the *Scottish Daily Record*. He dedicates this book of largely vintage Scottish jokes to the Unknown Aberdonian.

Also available:

THE OFFICIAL IRISH JOKE BOOK

THE OFFICIAL IRISH JOKE BOOK No. 3

Edited by Max Hodes

The Official Scottish Joke Book

Illustrated by Lorne Brown

Futura Publications Limited
A Futura Book

A Futura Book

First published in Great Britain by
Futura Publications Limited in 1978

ISBN 0 7088 1439 5

Printed in Great Britain by
Hazell Watson & Viney Ltd
Aylesbury, Bucks

Futura Publications Limited
110 Warner Road
Camberwell, London SE5

McPherson was just back from his holiday in the big city.

'Aye, London's a grand place,' he said, 'but they've some right queer customs. Every night they banged on my bedroom in that hotel – banging on the door, the wall, even the ceiling and floor. Sometimes I could hardly hear my bagpipes!'

* * *

Saturday night after Wembley, and Big Tam was set on by three London thugs. He fought them for three hours, but in the end they got all the cash he had left – 75p.

'Blimey,' said the one with the black eye, 'it's lucky he didn't have a quid – he'd have killed us!'

* * *

At the Rangers-Celtic game, Willie was annoyed at the way the man in front ducked his head every time a beer can sailed overhead.

'Don't be so nervous,' he said. 'If your name's on it, you'll get it.'

'That's just it,' said the man. 'My name's McEwan!'

* * *

5

When the *Titanic* sank, an Aberdeen
newspaper carried the headline
'Aberdeen Man Drowns'.

*　　*　　*

'A penny for your thoughts,' said Jean to
Jock, after a long silence.
'I'm just thinking about this morning's
work,' said Jock.
Another lengthy silence, and Jean said:
'What are you thinking about now?'
Replied Jock: 'I'm just thinking you
never gave me that penny yet . . .'

*　　*　　*

The tramp in Edinburgh approached a
kilted Highlander and said in a strong
English accent: 'Could you spare me a
fiver for me fare back to England?'
'That I can,' said the Highlander.
'Here's £20 – take another three back
with you!'

*　　*　　*

Jock is at the first tee. 'Are you any good
at finding golf balls?' he asks the caddy.
'Aye,' came the dour reply.
'Well,' says Jock, 'away and find one and
we'll get started . . .'

*　　*　　*

Mary was worried about redundancies in the shipyard where her husband worked, so she went to see the foreman. 'Who's being paid off this week?' she asked.

'Just six fitters,' replied the foreman.

'Thank God for that,' said Mary, 'My Willie's only five foot three!'

* * *

Said the Englishman to the boastful Scot: 'Take away your mountains, glens and lochs, and what have you got?'

'England,' replied the Scot.

* * *

Archie went with five Englishmen for a drink. The first round was six halves of whisky and six pints, and Archie's eyes widened when he saw the meagre change from a fiver.

Next round, he said: 'I'll just have a Horlicks, thanks.' He said the same for the third round, and so on.

When it came to HIS round, he was fast asleep.

* * *

Says Jessie to Jean: 'My goodness, Jean, it must be five years since I saw you last. You're looking an awful lot older.'
'Is that so?' replies Jean. 'I wouldn't have known you if it wasn't for your coat!'

*   *   *

At Sandy's 109th birthday party, a reporter asked him what kept him going. 'The thought of the funeral expenses,' said Sandy sadly.

*   *   *

Why did they make 50p pieces that shape? So you can fit a spanner to get one off an Aberdonian.

*   *   *

Two lads came to an Aberdonian's door collecting for a new swimming pool. He gave them a bucket of water.

*   *   *

Did you hear about the Aberdonian cleaning the windows in his high-rise flat? He accidentally dropped a 50p piece and was down the stairs so quickly it hit him on the head.

* * *

Then there were two Aberdonians who bet a pound on who could stay under water the longest. They both drowned.

* * *

A woman went to the cemetery to see her husband's grave. 'What's his name?' asked an attendant.
'Angus McSporran,' said the widow.
'Sorry,' replied the attendant, 'we don't have an Angus McSporran here, only a Jessie McSporran.'
'That's him,' said the widow. 'He put everything in his wife's name.'

* * *

Under a 'Smoking can damage your health' warning on a cigarette advertisement in Edinburgh, someone added: 'Inhale and farewell.'

*   *   *

Spare a thought for the Scottish football fan who lost all his luggage moments after stepping off the train at Euston. The cork fell out.

*   *   *

A footballer called Harry Haddock played full-back for Clyde.
One Saturday morning, two fans were discussing the team's chances.
One asked: 'What's the team today?'
His friend replied: 'Oh, the usual – ten hams and a haddie . . .'

*   *   *

The rich widow needed a blood transfusion, so a Scots donor saved her life. She was so grateful, she gave him £100.

But, after a relapse she needed another one and this time gave the donor £50. The third time he saved her life, she had so much Scots blood in her veins that she just thanked him very much.

*   *   *

Did you hear about the Aberdonian who went to a plastic surgeon? He wanted a new handle for his bucket.

*   *   *

At a football match, the Dumbarton keeper had just let in his fourth soft goal. 'Ach, catch it, pal,' cried a wag. 'It won't bite ye – its mouth is laced up!'

*   *   *

Old Sandy was dying. Tenderly, his wife Maggie knelt by his bedside and asked: 'Anything I can get you, Sandy?' No reply.
'Have ye no' a last wish, Sandy?'
Faintly, came the answer . . . 'a wee bit of yon boiled ham.'
'Wheesht, man,' said Maggie, 'ye ken fine that's for the funeral.'

*   *   *

The Kirkcaldy undertaker sent a telegram to the bereaved man, telling him his mother-in-law had died and asking whether he wanted her embalmed, cremated, or buried.
Back came the reply: 'All three – tak' nae chances.'

*   *   *

'McDougall's dead. He fell into a vat of whisky.'
'What a shame. Was it a quick death?'
'I don't think so. He came out twice to go to the bathroom!'

*   *   *

Did you hear about the Glasgow sawmill worker who didn't know he'd lost two fingers till he said goodnight to his foreman?

*　　*　　*

Then there was the cannibal who went to Ibrox Park to watch Rangers and Motherwell. He 8-3.

*　　*　　*

First Linwood car worker: 'I see the daffodils are out.' His mate: 'Do you think that will affect us?'

*　　*　　*

Two Celtic fans left a game and saw a policeman with a dog controlling the crowds. Said one: 'That's the first time I've ever seen a blind policeman.'

*　　*　　*

A policeman saw a boy walking along a
Glasgow street covered in feathers.
'How did you get feathers all over you?'
asked the policeman.
The boy replied: 'I was out with a bird.'

* * *

A Glasgow man went to the Labour
Exchange. The Pakistani clerk asked
him if he was looking for work (yes)
and had he any prospects of a job (no).
Said the Pakistani: 'Have you thought
about emigrating?'

* * *

A stranger in Glasgow was trying to get
a bus to Auchenshuggle. He asked a
newsvendor, who said: 'Go along to the
bus stop on the left and get a No. 18. If
you can't get one, catch two No. 9's.'

* * *

Graffiti on a loo in Glasgow's Central
Station: 'If you're putting toilet water on
your hair, mind you don't bang your
head on the seat.'

* * *

Hamish, on holiday in London, was having a furious argument with the bus conductor. 'I tell you the fare's only 10p,' he yelled.

'And I'm telling you it's 15p,' said the conductor. Then he lost his temper and, as they crossed a bridge, slung Hamish's suitcase into the Thames.

'By God,' shouted Hamish, 'ye've gone too far. First ye try to rob me with my fare, and now ye've drowned ma wee boy!'

* * *

Maggie was dying and called for her husband and said: 'At the funeral, I want you to ride in the second coach with my brother.'

Jock complained that he had hated his brother-in-law for years, but the wife insisted that it was her last wish.

'All right,' agreed Jock, 'but it'll spoil my day.'

* * *

Did you hear about the last wish of the henpecked husband of a houseproud Edinburgh wife? He asked to have his ashes scattered on the carpet.

* * *

It was a terrible winter – three months of unbroken blizzards.
McTavish hadn't been seen in the village for weeks, so a Red Cross rescue team struggled to his remote croft at the head of the glen. It was completely buried – only the chimney was showing.
'McTavish,' they shouted down the chimney. 'Are you there?'
'Wha's that?' came the answer.
'It's the Red Cross,' they called.
'Go away,' shouted McTavish. 'I bought a flag last year!'

* * *

Then there was the Inverness man who bought his mother-in-law a chair but had to send it back. He had nowhere to plug it in.

* * *

Jock's mother-in-law, who was most difficult to please, gave him two ties for Christmas.
To humour her, he put one on and went downstairs to dinner.
She looked at the tie and snarled: 'Whit's the matter? Do you no' like the ither one?'

*　　*　　*

A woman comes for a holiday in Aberdeen, and her landlady gives her fish for breakfast, lunch and tea.
After a week of this, she goes to a fortune-teller, who tells her she'll shortly meet a tall, dark stranger.
'I hope,' said the holidaymaker, 'that he's a butcher.'

*　　*　　*

Said a football fan of his favourite centre-forward: 'I hear Juventus are after him.' 'Aye,' said his friend Jock, 'and Fray Bentos are after the rest.'

*　　*　　*

Commonwealth Games gold medallist
Lachie Stewart was running round
Hampden Park before a Scotland-
England game.
Said a fan: 'Is that not typical? He gets a
medal and a lap of honour for doing
10,000 metres.
'My brother did one meter and got six
months.'

*   *   *

Did you hear about the woman who
walked into the housing factor's office
with a five-pound note in each ear? The
assistant said: 'It's Mrs McPherson. Ten
pounds in arrears again . . .'

*   *   *

Then there was the wee boy who was
asked by his teacher where Pakistan
was. 'It canny be far away, miss,' he
replied, 'because Ali goes hame fur his
dinner.'

*   *   *

Another wee boy came from the Gorbals. His family were really hard-up. One day, to his surprise, his father gave him 10p. When he came back . . . they had moved.

*   *   *

A friend called to comfort the bereaved wife and found her bright and cheerful. 'I thought you'd have been full of grief,' said the friend.
'Well,' replied the widow, 'he may have been the father of my bairns, but he wisnae a blood relation.'

*   *   *

Two Partick Thistle supporters were on fire-watching duty in the last war. During an air raid, they took shelter in the doorway of a pub near the ground. When a bomb came screaming down and exploded just behind the pub, one said to the other: 'As usual – over the bar'.

*   *   *

First football manager: 'You're invited to a party I'm giving tomorrow night.'
Second football manager: 'I can't manage.'
First football manager: 'I know – but come just the same!'

* * *

A Glasgow man was walking across the city's suspension bridge. He saw an old man struggling in the water, gasping: 'Help! I cannae swim.'
Replied the man: 'Ah cannae play golf, but ah don't shout about it!'

* * *

As Jock lay dying, he heard his tight-fisted sons discussing the funeral arrangements.
They went on and on about the best ways to keep down the funeral expenses.
Finally, Jock called out: 'Just give me over ma troosers, an' I'll walk tae the cemetery myself!'

* * *

An American visitor asked in an Edinburgh shop for the McIntyre tartan. The shopkeeper said he hadn't any but offered him the Dunlop tartan instead. The American protested this wouldn't do, to which the shopkeeper replied: 'After all, Dunlops have been *makin' tyres* for years!'

*   *   *

The scene was a sparsely-filled Hampden Park, during a mediocre game between Queen's Park and Albion Rovers.
A shout of 'Waken up, Rovers!' was quickly answered by one of 'Waken up, Queen's!'
To which a third raucous voice was heard to shout: 'Ach, ye cannae waken the dead!'

*   *   *

News flash: Fighting between Rangers and Celtic supporters was interrupted for 90 minutes today, when the pitch was invaded by 22 players.

*   *   *

A man went to watch Partick Thistle.
He gave the man at the turnstile a
pound note and said: 'Two, please.'
'Forwards or defenders?' asked the
attendant.

*　　*　　*

A wee Fife boy wrote to Father
Christmas, c/o the North Pole, and said
he wanted £5 to buy presents for his
parents and little brother, because they
had no money.
The letter was opened by one of the staff
at the PO sorting office. He was so
touched that he and his friends had a
whipround and sent the boy £3.
Then another letter arrived from the
boy: 'Thanks for the money you sent,
but those thieving swine at the Post
Office stole £2.'

*　　*　　*

Did you hear about the Aberdonian who
tried to buy a stick of rock at Blackpool
with a Barclay Card?

*　　*　　*

There were puzzled frowns in Perth
Sheriff Court when a lawyer told the
sheriff his client earned his living as a
saint prayer.
'A what?' asked the sheriff. 'Sorry, your
honour,' came the reply. 'I meant to say
paint sprayer.'

* * *

Then there was the Aberdonian who had
a rough finish to the bottom of his
teacups to make visitors think there was
sugar in them.

* * *

After the 1967 European Cup Final in
Portugal, a Celtic supporter was hitch-
hiking on the outskirts of Lisbon.
A car drew up and a sympathetic
Scottish voice asked if he would like a
lift.
'Where are you going?' asked the hitch-
hiker.
'Edinburgh,' replied the car driver.
'No use,' said the hiker. 'I'm going to
Glasgow.'

* * *

Celtic fans caused so much confusion after a European Cup game in Milan that seating lists for the return flights were disregarded.

Fans were put on board on a first come-first served basis, including one who was carried on asleep after being spotted in the departure lounge.

His thanks were more abusive than effusive when he woke up as the plane circled Glasgow. He had driven to Milan in his own car.

*   *   *

Disgruntled worker: 'I've been here five years, doing the work of three men for one man's wage, and it's time I had a rise.'

Employer: 'I canna give you that, but just tell me the names o' the other two men an' I'll sack them.'

*   *   *

The local train stopped at a station long
enough for the passengers to stretch
their legs.
Sniffing the pure, clean air with
appreciation, a passenger said to the
guard: 'Invigorating, isn't it?'
'No,' he replied. 'Inverurie.'

*   *   *

'I hear your son's an undertaker. I
thought you said he was a doctor.'
'I said nothing o' the kind. I said he
followed the medical profession.'

*   *   *

An Aberdonian, spying a penny in
Piccadilly, stopped to pick it up and was
run over by a bus.
The coroner's verdict: 'Death through
natural causes.'

*   *   *

A thirsty Scot went into an English local and ordered a pint of beer. Looking thoughtfully at the head on it, he asked: 'Do you think you could get a nip of rum into this glass?'
'Certainly, sir,' replied the barman.
'In that case,' said the Scot, 'perhaps you'd just top it up with beer.'

*   *   *

Jock was helping at the birth by holding an oil lamp. When the doctor produced twins, Angus disappeared with the light.
'Here, come back with the lamp,' called the doctor. 'I think there's another!'
'Not me,' replied Angus. 'It's the light that's attracting them!'

*   *   *

The minister was sharing a rail compartment with a Scot the worse of drink, who insisted on talking.
'Please don't speak to me,' said the minister. 'You're drunk.'
'Drunk?' replied the Scot. 'You're worse than me – you've got your collar on back to front.'

*   *   *

Three times Jessie brought Sandy to the manse, hoping to be made man and wife, but each time the minister refused because of the groom-to-be's intoxication.

'Why do you persist in bringing him to me in such a state?' asked the minister.

'Please, Reverend,' explained Jessie, 'he'll no' come when he's sober.'

*　　*　　*

Jock went into a shop to buy a pocket knife. 'Here's the very thing,' said the shopkeeper, 'four blades and a corkscrew.'

'Tell me,' said Jock, 'you haven't one with four corkscrews and a blade, have you?'

*　　*　　*

An Aberdonian was ill with scarlet fever. 'Send for my creditors,' he said. 'I can give them something at last.'

*　　*　　*

New minister: 'Well, Angus, what did you think of my sermon?'
Angus: 'Real good, sir. We knew nothing aboot sin till ye came here.'

* * *

After a convivial evening, two Scots were homeward-bound on the train.
'Nationalisation,' said Willie, 'is the best thing that's ever happened to the railways.'
'You're right,' said his friend. 'You're going to London and I'm going to Glasgow, an' we're both on the same train!'

* * *

Jock: 'How much for a trip across in the ferry?'
Ferryman: 'One penny, sir.'
Jock: 'Do y'have any excursions?'

* * *

It was cold on the upper deck and the captain was concerned for the comfort of his passengers.

He called down: 'Is there a mackintosh down there big enough to keep two young lassies warm?'

'No, skipper,' came the reply, 'but there's a MacPherson willing to try.'

* * *

Inspector: 'Tell the foreman when you see him this trench is dangerous.'

Jock: 'He knows – I'm diggin' him oot.'

* * *

'I hear you're a great believer in free speech.'

'I am that, Angus.'

'Well, do you mind if I use your phone?'

* * *

Magistrate: 'Where were you born?'

Prisoner: 'Dundee, sir.'

Magistrate: 'Were you brought up there?'

Prisoner: 'Aye, many a time.'

* * *

'It was like this,' said Donald. 'I was teaching the wife to drive, and the brakes failed when we came down the hill.'
'What did you tell her?'
'Try and hit something cheap!'

* * *

A woman and a man from Aberdeen were stranded on a desert island after a shipwreck. Their clothes were in rags and their food running out.
'I suppose it could always be worse,' said the woman.
'Oh, aye, it could,' agreed the Aberdonian. 'I might have bought a return ticket.'

* * *

'Any complaints?' asked the prison governor.
'Aye,' replied Sandy, 'the walls are no' built to scale.'

* * *

'Would you care to join the Anti-Tipping Society? The subscription is only 5p a year.'
Aberdonian: 'No, no – It'd be cheaper tae tip.'

* * *

'Aha,' said the Customs officer, producing a bottle of whisky. 'I thought you said your case contained nothing but clothes.'
'Correct,' said Sandy. 'That's my nightcap.'

* * *

Maggie put 'Rest In Peace' on her hubby's tombstone. But when she found he had left her nothing in his will, she told the stonemason to add the words 'Till I come.'

* * *

'Dad, you promised me 10p if I was top of the class, and I am.'
'Well, here you are, but don't study so hard – it's no' good for ye.'

* * *

A Scot with a bottle was boasting at a football match about his own prowess at the game.
As the level of the contents went down, the man next to him said: 'I can see you're a fine dribbler, but you're no' much use at passing!'

*　*　*

He: 'Drinkin' makes you look bonnie.'
She: 'But I haven't been drinking.'
He: 'No, but I have.'

*　*　*

A Scot from a lonely Highland glen paid his first visit to London and was hailed by a driver 'Taxi, sir?'
'Nae thanks,' he replied.
After seeing the sights, he went on to Brighton, where he was again greeted by the familiar, 'Taxi, sir?'
'Look,' he shouted, 'I said "no" in London and I meant it. Now please stop following me about.'

*　*　*

The minister got a phone call from the
station to tell him that a parcel awaited
collection.
'Good,' he said. 'It's some books I
ordered from Edinburgh.'
Station master: 'Well, you'd better hurry
up. They're leakin'.'

*   *   *

'And how's your man, Mrs Johnstone?'
'Ach, he's back in the pits and it's killing
him – but thank goodness it's
permanent.'

*   *   *

Jean was fed up with her husband's
drunken habits, so she decided to teach
him a lesson. She wrapped herself in a
sheet and set off to meet him.
'I am the Devil,' she greeted him, 'and
I've come to claim my own!'
'Let me shake your hand,' beamed
Sandy. 'I married your sister!'

*   *   *

'I got a shock when I heard of Willie's
death. What did he die of?'
'I'm no' sure, but I believe it was
nothing serious.'

* * *

Golfing mates were at the wet and windy
funeral of their friend Sandy.
'One thing,' said Jock, 'he wouldn't have
played today, anyway.'

* * *

The train stopped at an outlandish
station, and a passenger asked the guard
if he had time to nip out for a dram.
'There's only one way to be sure,' said
the guard, 'perhaps I could come wi' ye.'

* * *

An old Scot was sitting in the railway
waiting room enjoying a smoke.
Said the porter: 'Can ye no' see that
notice, "No Smoking Allowed"?'
'Aye,' said the Scot, 'but how can I keep
all your rules? There's another notice
that says "Wear Tight-Fit Corsets".'

* * *

38

'Father, teacher says I've tae get a new atlas.'
'Aye, well, you can wait till the world's more settled.'

* * *

Campbell and Macdonald had been good friends for years, but one evening Macdonald was very quiet. 'What's wrong?' asked Campbell.
'Well, if you must know,' said Macdonald, 'it's that terrible massacre of the Macdonalds by the Campbells at Glencoe that's on my mind.'
'But that was hundreds of years ago,' Campbell pointed out.
'Maybe, maybe,' replied Macdonald, 'but I only heard about it yesterday.'

* * *

Yank: 'Gee, son, you're very small.'
Sandy: 'Aye, I was brought up on
condensed milk and shortbread.'

*   *   *

Then there was the Scot carrying a
parcel of whisky who crashed to the
ground. He cautiously examined a wet
patch, smelt it, and said: 'Thank God
it's blood.'

*   *   *

Sandy was due to speak in the village
hall, when his false teeth broke.
'Don't worry,' said one of the platform
party, 'I've a friend who'll fix you up.'
Off he went and returned with a set of
dentures, which fitted perfectly.
'That's a wonderful dentist,' said Sandy
later, 'to fix me up at such short notice.'
'He's no dentist,' came the reply. 'He's
the undertaker.'

*   *   *

'I sometimes think you only married me, Angus, because Uncle Archie left me £10,000.'
'Nonsense, woman, I wouldn't have cared *who* left it tae you!'

* * *

After months of toil in his garden, Willie was at last seeing some of the fruits of his labour.
As he was admiring the display of flowers and vegetables, the minister passed. 'Well, Willie,' he said, 'you and the Creator have done a grand job in this garden.'
'Maybe so,' replied Willie, 'but you should have seen it when He had it to Himsel'!'

* * *

Did you hear about the superstitious Scot who was run over by a lorry-load of white heather? The lorry-driver swerved to avoid a black cat.

* * *

Doorman at Burns Supper: 'What do you mean – you've come to propose the Immortal Memory and forgotten your ticket?'

* * *

Old Jock, who seldom left his croft, was visiting Edinburgh Zoo. 'This animal,' the guide informed him, 'is a native of Africa. Over there's a native of India.' When he came to the kangaroo enclosure, the guide said, 'And here's a native of Australia.'
'Guid heavens!' cried Jock, with dismay. 'My daughter's married to one of them!'

* * *

Three Scots were in church one Sunday, when the minister made a strong charity appeal. 'I hope everyone in the congregation will give £1 or more,' he said.
As the collection plate got nearer the three apprehensive Scots – one of them fainted and the other two carried him out.

* * *

An old worthy at Inverness was having
trouble with his hens, which kept
wandering on to a nearby railway line.
In desperation, he nailed a poster to the
hen-house door giving a list of the local
trains.
'Well, if you get run over now,' he
muttered as he left, 'it's your ain
damned fault!'

*　　*　　*

'Whit's courage, dad?'
'Refusing tae tip in a restaurant.'
'Whit's discretion?'
'Not going back.'

*　　*　　*

Then there was the Aberdonian who
went to a fancy-dress ball as Napoleon –
so he could keep his hand on his wallet.

*　　*　　*

Someone told Harry Lauder that his native country was raising £20,000 to erect a statue of him.

'Give me the £20,000,' said Lauder, 'and ah'll stand on the pedestal maself!'

.   *   *   *

Angus had a 15-mile walk for his provisions, which included a box of matches. To his dismay, he found they would not light.

Back he went next day to complain to the local grocer, who took one from the box, drew it across the seat of his trousers, and got it to light first time.

'There you are, Angus,' he said, 'there's nothing wrang with these matches.'

'And who,' asked Angus, 'is going tae walk 15 miles to light his matches on *your* troosers?'

*   *   *

Guide at Scots castle: 'This castle has stood for 500 years. Not a stone has been touched, nothing repaired, nothing altered, or replaced.'
Glaswegian visitor: 'Must hiv the same landlord as us.'

*   *   *

After the blacksmith had shown some English visitors over the battlefield at Bannockburn, they clubbed together and offered him £2.50.
'No, no, keep your money,' he replied, 'this affair has cost ye enough already!'

*   *   *

'Ah tell ye ah won't have this room,' protested the old lady from Banff to the hotel porter. 'Ah'm no' paying guid money for a closet wi' a folding bed—'
'Get in, madam, get in,' said the porter wearily. 'This is the lift.'

*   *   *

'It was so cold,' said the Aberdonian, 'I almost got married.'

* * *

Comedian Les Dawson: 'I'm very proud of my Scots extraction. I once had a tooth out in Arbroath.'

* * *

Then there was the minister who bought a used car and didn't have the vocabulary to run it.

* * *

An Aberdonian's definition of a wonderful after-dinner speaker: Someone who always says, 'Give me the bill.'

* * *

'I'm sorry,' said the Job Centre boss, 'we have very few Scots on our books. I understand you want only Scots?'
Employer: 'Well, if we cannae get Scots, we're prepared to accept a few superior English.'

*　　*　　*

Willie to servant girl, on finding his wife had passed away during the night:
'Maggie – ye need boil only one egg this mornin'!'

*　　*　　*

Famous (Aberdonian) Last Words:
'Well, if he won't dim his, ah won't dim mine!'

*　　*　　*

An absent-minded Aberdonian professor liked to join his students for a game of cards. All put 10p in the kitty, except the professor.

Not liking to tell him directly, the students pretended to argue among themselves as to which had not paid his stake.

The professor listened for a while, then withdrew one of the 10p pieces from the kitty.

'If you lot are going to quarrel,' he said, 'I'm taking my money back.'

*   *   *

A Yugoslav girl, working for a Forfar firm, had little knowledge of English. Writing home, she painstakingly copied the address off the notice at the factory gate.

In due course, the reply arrived addressed to: Lockwoods Foods Ltd, Trespassers Will Be Prosecuted, Forfar.

*   *   *

Rivalry has always existed between Edinburgh, Scotland's capital, and Glasgow.
A charity raffle in Glasgow offered the following prizes: 1st prize: One week in Edinburgh. 2nd prize: Two weeks in Edinburgh.

*   *   *

Calling at a friend's house in Glasgow, you're liable to be greeted with, 'Come on in and have your tea.'
In Edinburgh, the greeting is likely to be, 'Come in – you'll have had your tea.'

*   *   *

Sheriff to accused in Fife court: 'Pig-stealing is far too prevalent in the burgh. Unless an example is made in this case, none of us will be safe.'

*   *   *

The Russians sent a submarine into
Aberdeen with instruction to their
agents to contact a Mr Smith in Victoria
Road, Torry – traditionally a close-
mouthed sector of the city.
The agents found a Mr Smith and gave
the password – 'It's a braw bricht
moonlicht nicht the nicht.'
To be told by the occupier: 'Naw, naw,
it's nae me ye want – it's Smith the spy
that stays across the road.'

*   *   *

Jock, who had a stammer, went into a
pet shop and tried to ask for half a
pound of budgerigar seed. But he
couldn't get the words out.
Day after day, he went back but failed to
get beyond: 'H-h-have you g-g-got h-h-
hauf a pound of b-b-budge—?'
Finally, the shopkeeper caught on.
'What you want is half a pound of
budgie seed,' he said.
'T-t-too late,' replied Jock. 'He's d-d-
died o' starvation.'

*   *   *

'Well, Angus,' said the chemist, 'did that mudpack I suggested improve your wife's appearance?'
'It did for a couple of days,' replied Angus, 'but then it wore off.'

*   *   *

A small cargo vessel was unloading timber at a west coast of Scotland pier. The skipper, directing operations, noticed that Donald was taking two planks at a time and Archie only one. 'Don't you see, Archie, that Donald is carrying two planks at a time.'
'Indeed I do,' replied Archie. 'In fact, I was meaning to speak to him about it myself.'

*   *   *

Old lady: 'Tell me – is anything worn under your kilt?'
Jock: 'I assure you, madam, everything's in perfect working order.'

*   *   *

The message boy was on his rounds in Melrose. Delivering to a new resident, he was asked his name. 'Walter Scott, sir,' came the reply.

'Indeed,' said the newcomer, 'that's a very well-known name in these parts.'

'So it should be,' retorted the boy, 'I've been delivering here for aboot three years!'

*   *   *

'Is Wullie in?' asked Andra.

'Aye, he's in,' replied the wife.

'Can I see him?'

'No, ye canna.'

'It's on a bit o' business.'

'Well, ye canna see him. He's deid.'

'Was it sudden?'

'Aye, very sudden.'

'Did he happen to say onything about a pot o' green paint before he slipped away?'

*   *   *

Tramp in Aberdeen: 'Will ye give me tuppence for a bed, missus?'
Wife: 'Let me think. Bring it up and we'll see what it's like.'

*   *   *

'Now, Angus,' said Jock from the railway carriage window in Aberdeen, 'if anything should happen to Grannie, remember to send me a wire. And dinna forget you can get eight words for 50p.'
In due course, Angus's message arrived: 'Grannie passed away today. Aberdeen 2, Rangers 1.'

*   *   *

On her first visit to St Andrews, a young
girl had a golf lesson from a local
instructor.

Instead of starting with a driver, the
teacher gave her a mashie and instructed
her to play for a hole some 60 yards
away.

The girl hit the ball towards the target,
and, to her surprise and delight, the ball
finished in the hole. 'How was that?' she
asked.

The instructor shook his head. 'Naw,
naw,' he said. 'That'll no dae at all.
Your grip's all wrong . . .'

*　　*　　*

In the early rounds of the Scottish Cup,
lowly Vale of Atholl were drawn to meet
Rangers at Ibrox Park, Glasgow.

For those unable to make the trip to
Glasgow, it was arranged that the final
score would be telegraphed to the local
Post Office.

In due course, the telegram arrived, and
the Postmaster announced '15-0' to the
waiting crowd.

There was a stunned silence among the
supporters, broken by one brave voice –
'Who for?'

*   *   *

'Aye,' the golf member was explaining,
'I asked him what his handicap was, and
he said he was a poor 18 man who
hadn't played for six months.

'I told him I hadn't handled a club for
over a year, and was crippled with
lumbago.

'We agreed to play for 50p. And believe
it or not, I had to dae two under fours
tae beat him!'

*   *   *

Jock, a caddie of the old school, was employed by a distinguished visitor to St Andrews. Anxious to improve his game, the visitor promised Jock a bottle of Scotch if he broke 100 strokes.

By the time he got to the 18th tee, the visitor needed only a five to achieve the elusive 99. But his 98th stroke finished 15 yards beyond the hole.

'Well done, sir,' said Jock, rushing forward to pick up the ball. 'Anybody would give you that one!'

* * *

A Deeside wife listened for a whole evening to the jokes and patter of Billy Connolly without a hint of a smile.

Next day she confided to a friend: 'He's a great comic. It was all I could do tae keep from laughing.'

* * *

'Are you the man that dived into the Clyde to pull my wee boy out of the water?'

'Aye.'

'Well, where's his cap?'

* * *

Then there was the Aberdeen soldier who said nothing to his wife about winning the V.C. because it was her turn to write.

*   *   *

The English visitor to the Ross-shire moors was so confident of his shooting powers that he promised to give Donald, his ghillie, 5p for every bird he missed. Telling the story to his pals in the pub, Donald added: 'Aye, it was a grand day's sport. Anither blank cartridge an' I'd have had a pound!'

*   *   *

'Anything important today, skipper?' shouted the piermaster.
'Nothin' at all,' replied the skipper. 'Just two bulls and a minister.'

*   *   *

When Willie retired from the railway after 50 years' service, the company presented him with an old coach to keep in his garden as a memento.

One wet day, his friends found him sitting on the step of the coach, smoking his pipe, with an old sack over his shoulders to keep out the rain.

'Hullo, Willie,' said his pals, 'why are ye no' inside on a day like this?'

'Can ye no' see,' replied Willie, with a nod towards the coach. 'They sent me a non-smoker!'

*　　*　　*

Old Annie consulted the doctor about her stomach. 'It's nothing to worry about,' he said, 'just a bit of wind.'

'Jist a bit of wind?' replied Annie. 'Did ye no ken it was wind that blew doon the Tay Bridge?'

*　　*　　*

The Bible teacher had given the children
a graphic account of the hardships of
Mary and Joseph, how they could find
no room at the inn and had to take
refuge in a stable.
At the start of the next Scripture lesson,
a small boy raised his hand. 'Please,
miss,' he asked, 'is there any word of yon
folk that were lookin' for a hoose?'

*　　*　　*

Did you hear about the woman who
wrote off for a cheap Scottish holiday?
They sent her a Highlander on a
tandem.

*　　*　　*

Jock calls on his friend Sandy and finds
him stripping off the wallpaper.
'Aye, Sandy – I see ye're decorating.'
'No, Jock – ah'm moving!'

*　　*　　*

Then there was the Aberdonian who
sold his son his ring on his deathbed.
The son paid by cheque.

*　　*　　*

Another Aberdonian died and left his money to the Unknown Soldier's widow.

* * *

'My first wife drowned. We were standing beside the wishing-well and she fell in.' – Comedian Hector Nicol.

* * *

Sandy went into a restaurant and ate a businessman's lunch. The businessman was furious.

* * *

An 18-inch midget from Glasgow went to the doctor. 'What seems to be the trouble?' asked the doctor.
Replied the midget: 'I'm not too fit.'

* * *

An Edinburgh man, short of cigarettes, went into a Chinese restaurant and asked for 20 No. 6.
He came out with 3 cwt of fried rice.

* * *

A new restaurant offered £100 to anyone
who ordered a dish they could not
supply.
An Aberdonian went in and asked for
giraffe's kneecaps on toast.
The waiter returned with £100, saying,
'You win – we're out of bread.'

*   *   *

They say the police go about in two's in
Easterhouse, Glasgow. And that's inside
the police office.

*   *   *

Comedian Clem Dane says he comes
from a long line of boxers, all except his
uncle. He was a cocker spaniel.

*   *   *

Wife: 'I had to leave the car. There was
water in the carburettor.'
Husband: 'Where is it now?'
Wife: 'In the Clyde.'

*   *   *

Jock staggered in at 5 a.m. undressed, tiptoed upstairs with his clothes over his arm, and found he was on a bus.

*   *   *

Sandy walked into a pub and drank McEwan's beer. McEwan nearly knocked his head off.

*   *   *

Billy Connolly to heckler: 'You should be on the stage. There's one leavin' in three minutes.'

*   *   *

Jock to engine driver: 'Can ye no' go any quicker?'
Engine driver: 'I'm no' allowed tae leave the train.'

*   *   *

My wife ran away with my best friend, whoever he is. – Ronnie Corbett.

*   *   *

Then there was the Dundee man who complained he went into a store for a straw hat and got felt.

* * *

McTavish: 'How much will it cost to take me and my luggage to the station?'
Taxi-driver: 'Fifty pence. The luggage goes for nothing.'
McTavish: 'Right – take my luggage and I'll walk.'

* * *

The Scot is built to wear the kilt
With Caledonian ardour,
He's bold, I'm told, though winds
blow cold,
Sometimes round Auchterarder.
                              —Anon.

* * *

McGregor was asked by a friend during an argument: 'Have you ever heard of my honesty being questioned?'
'Questioned?' came the reply. 'I've never even heard it mentioned.'

* * *

Nowadays grannies don't want a wee home in the Highlands. They want a big house at the bingo. – Comedian Johnny Beattie.

*   *   *

A haggis looks like a football. You don't know whether to eat it or kick it. After you've eaten it, you wish you'd kicked it.

*   *   *

Then there was the Aberdonian whose family were never cold in winter. He'd eat a cough lozenge and breathe all over them.

*   *   *

Two old men were passing a graveyard. 'You've a bad cough, Donald,' said one. 'Aye,' said the other, 'but there's a lot of folk in there that would be glad of a cough like mine.'

*   *   *

I may be under the affluence of incohol,
but I'm not so think as you drunk I am.
– Will Fyffe.

*   *   *

Then there was the Inverness railway
guard whose wife put a half-pea in his
whistle, and he only got the train half-
started.

*   *   *

Passenger, to train driver: 'Can I get out
and pick a few flowers while the train's
in motion?'
Driver: 'If you look out, you'll see there's
no flowers on this embankment.'
Passenger: 'That's all right – I've
brought a packet of seeds.'

*   *   *

There was a young man of Uphall,
Who went to a fancy-dress ball.
He thought he would risk it,
And go as a biscuit,
But a dog ate him up in the hall.

*   *   *

Mrs Macgregor answered a knock at the door. 'Could you give anything to the Inebriates' Home?' asked the caller. 'Come back at eleven,' she replied, 'and I'll give ye Jock.'

*　　*　　*　　.

An Aberdonian was walking along Princes Street, Edinburgh, when a young man approached him and asked for a match. The Aberdonian produced a box of matches and handed them over. 'That's perfect,' said the young man. 'You're in luck. I'm on a sales-promotion campaign, and my job is to give £5 to the first man who shows me a box of these particular matches.' He gave the astonished Aberdonian a fiver and walked away.

The Aberdonian looked at the money for a moment in bewilderment, then cried: 'Hi, come back! I knew there was a catch in it – you're away wi' my matches!'

*　　*　　*

The minister was walking along the street when he saw a solemn procession of small boys marching along the kerbside. 'What's this game, sonny?' he asked the boy in front.

'It's a funeral,' replied the boy.

'Oh,' said the minister, 'who's dead?'

'Don't ask me,' said the boy. 'I'm the horse.'

*   *   *

The minister thought it best to see home an elder who was the worse for drink. As they entered the house, the elder's wife shouted: 'Drunk again, John?' and the elder replied: 'Aye, an' ye'll never guess who I've been with.'

*   *   *

'Why worry? There are only two things to worry about – whether you're well or ill. If you're well, you've nothing to worry about. If you're ill, you've only two things to worry about – whether you're going to live or die.

'If you're going to live, you've nothing to worry about. If you're going to die, you've only two things to worry about – whether you're going up there or down there.

'If you're going up there, you've nothing to worry about. And if you're going down there, you'll be so busy shaking hands with all your friends, you'll have no time to worry!' – Comedian Lex McLean.

*   *   *

Jock admits his wife controls the children, the cat and the canary, but he can say what he likes to the goldfish.

*   *   *

'My wife kisses me every time I come hame.'
'Is that affection?'
'Naw – investigation.'

* * *

Judge: 'Do you know the penalty for bigamy?'
Sandy: 'Aye – twa mothers-in-law.'

* * *

Two young Aberdonians were sitting in a bus when a pretty girl came in and sat down near them.
'That's Maggie McPherson,' said one. 'I think I'll go and speak to her.'
'Dinna be in such a hurry,' said his pal. 'Wait till she's paid her fare.'

* * *

Sandy was about to take a tricky putt, when a funeral passed by. He stopped to stand with head uncovered until it had gone.

His opponent remarked: 'I didn't think you were as respectful as all that, Sandy.'

'Man, it was the least I could do,' came the reply. 'She was a good wife tae me.'

*　　*　　*

McTavish was so tired hearing jokes about mean Scots in a New York saloon that he stood drinks all round. He took a heart attack when he learned they had imagined he was an Irishman.

*　　*　　*

Maggie: 'Ye never bring me hame yon candy and flowers ye used to bring when we were courting.'

Jock: 'Naw, a man doesn't bait the hook after he's caught the fish.'

*　　*　　*

Teacher: 'Your homework sum was – "If a man walks four miles in one hour, how long will he take to walk 25 miles?" Why isn't it done?'

Boy: 'My father's no' back yet.'

*　　*　　*

Asked in his exam for a definition of water, Davie wrote: 'A colourless liquid that turns black when you put your hands in it.'

*　　*　　*

Passer-by: 'What's the lantern for?'

Watchman: 'So that folk won't fall over yon heap of stones in the dark.'

Passer-by: 'And what's the heap of stones for?'

Watchman: 'Tae hold up the lantern.'

*　　*　　*

'Who gave you that black eye, son?'

'Naebudy. Ah had tae fight for it.'

*　　*　　*

Beggar: 'I'm really an author. I wrote a book called "One hundred ways to earn money".'
Man: 'Then why are you begging?'
Beggar: 'This is one of the hundred ways.'

*   *   *

Then there was the Aberdonian who drowned in the Black Sea while filling his fountain pen.

*   *   *

Tonight we talk to a man who crossed a Gordon Highlander with a mousetrap and got a squeaky jockstrap.
And to a man who crossed a bulldog, a retriever and a Scots terrier and got a very strong dog that tosses the caber and then brings it back. – Ronnie Corbett.

*   *   *

What do you call a skeleton in a kilt? Boney Prince Charlie.

*   *   *

Sir Harry Lauder was said to take all his money out of the bank every year for a holiday. Then, when it had had a holiday, he put it all back.

*   *   *

Mrs McTavish told her husband she was expecting a party of guests. He immediately rose and hid all the umbrellas.
'Are you afraid the guests will steal your umbrellas?' she asked.
'Naw,' he replied, 'Ah'm afraid they'll recognise them.'

*   *   *

An Edinburgh teacher was checking the school meals list, noting which children were entitled to free dinners.
She asked Peter: 'Are you free?'
'No,' he replied, 'I'm five.'
'I mean do you get free dinners?'
'Naw, miss – only one!'

*   *   *

Then there was the Aberdonian who saved all his toys for his second childhood.

* * *

Jock (in the rough): 'What are ye lookin' at your watch for, caddie?'
Caddie: 'This is nae watch – it's a compass.'

* * *

A young Dundee couple were looking at a motor-cycle and sidecar in a showroom window.
'You could take me all sorts o' places if you had that,' said the girl.
'Na, na, lassie,' replied the lad, 'you be satisfied with the fine carriage nature gave ye.'

* * *

Then there was the Scot who went into a harness shop and asked for a single spur. 'If I get one side of the horse to go, the other side will have to come with it,' he explained.

* * *

The Scots are the only race I know who can limbo under lavatory doors. – Dave Allen.

*   *   *

Did you hear about McTavish? He's so mean he disconnects the little light every time he opens the fridge door.

*   *   *

Then there was the Scot who went into a tailor's and asked to see a suit. The Jewish proprietor came back with a nice Harris Tweed. 'Look at this,' he said, 'and it's *not* £50. Not even £40 – £30 and it's yours.'
The Scot examined it carefully. 'I wouldn't give you £25 for it – not even £20. My price is £18.'
'Right,' said the Jew. 'That's the way I like to do business – no haggling!'

*   *   *

Househunter: 'I thought you said there was a fitted kitchen?'
Sandy: 'Well, it's attached to the house, isn't it?'

*   *   *

Excavators in Aberdeen came on a Scottish penny, dated 1588. A few feet away, they unearthed three skeletons, all on their hands and knees.

*   *   *

The McDougalls were sitting in their kitchen when the gas stove blew out. It was the first time they'd been out together for 40 years.

*   *   *

A traveller from the Aberdeen Kilt Company found himself stranded in snowstorms in the Orkneys and wired his company for instructions. The reply came: 'Start summer holidays as of now'.

*   *   *

Old Angus stayed with a business friend in London and got very attached to the friend's golden retriever. The dog returned his affections and kicked up such a fuss when Angus was leaving that the Londoner insisted he be taken home as a gift.

'That's very good of you,' said Angus. 'As soon as I get back to Aberdeen, I'll send you the finest turkey you ever saw.' Several months passed and the pair met again. 'What happened to the turkey you promised to send me?' asked the friend. 'Ah forgot to tell ye,' replied Angus, 'it got well.'

* * *

'Well, Willie,' said Bob, 'and how do you like married life?'
'Not bad,' replied Willie, 'except that she's always ask, ask, asking for money.'
'And how much have you given her?'
'Oh, nothing yet.'

* * *

A Scot had just been appointed to a position in a big firm down south, and a friend, meeting him later, asked: 'Well, how do you like the English?'

'Well,' said the Scot, 'I haven't met any of them yet. You see, I only deal with the heads of departments.'

*   *   *

Houdini made one of his rare miscalculations when he fought his way out of a straitjacket and handcuffs from the top span of a big bridge in Scotland. But nobody turned up. 'Don't they like me here?' Houdini asked a city official. 'Oh, they like you all right,' replied the official, 'but you should never have performed on a toll bridge.'

*   *   *

McPherson, a commercial traveller, ran out of petrol on a lonely road in the Highlands and asked at the only farmhouse in sight: 'Can you put me up for the night?'

'Aye,' said the farmer, 'if you don't mind sharing a bed with my 18-year-old son.'

'My God,' gasped McPherson, 'I'm in the wrong joke!'

*   *   *

Everyone knows it was a Scotsman who invented the briefcase.

*   *   *

A middle-aged farmer from Peterhead married a pretty young thing and drove her home in his carriage after the reception.

Suddenly, the horse reared up on its hind legs. 'Whoa, there, lass!' he cautioned. 'That's once.'

A few minutes later, it shied again. 'Whoa, lass, dammit,' he yelled. 'That's twice!'

When the horse reared up for the third time, he picked up his gun and shot it dead.

His bride was horrified. 'You big bully,' she cried, 'just because a poor animal . . .'

'Whoa, there, lass!' he chided. 'That's once!'

*   *   *

Jean's first confinement produced triplets. With understandable pride, she told her friend this happened only once in every 200,000 times.

'My, my,' said her friend. 'It beats me how you ever found time to do any housework.'

*   *   *

Jock met his friend Sandy in the street. 'I wonder if you'd oblige me with a cigarette?' he asked.
'But I thought you'd stopped smoking,' said Andy.
'I've just reached the first stage,' explained Jock. 'I've stopped buying them.'

*   *   *

Talk about mean? Sandy went into the garden on Christmas Eve, fired off his shotgun, then told his children Father Christmas had committed suicide.

*   *   *

At the reunion of old friends, the Englishman brought a crate of beer, the Irishman brought a big cooked ham . . . and the Scotsman brought his brother.

*   *   *

Asked the secret of his long life, Angus explained: 'I make two rules. Never take whisky without water, and never take water without whisky.'

*　　*　　*

Jimmy had hitch-hiked to Wembley and back for the big game. 'Was it a big gate?' asked his pal. 'Aye,' replied Jimmy, 'the biggest I've ever climbed over.'

*　　*　　*

After seven daughters, Dougal had a son at last. 'Who does the wee fellow look like?' asked a friend. 'I haven't the faintest idea,' replied Dougal. 'We haven't looked at his face yet.'

*　　*　　*

Bob and Willie, their wives away, were all set for a good night. They bought two bottles of Malt and a 4lb sirloin steak. After a few drams they went into the kitchen to fry the steak, but it had gone. Seeing the cat licking its whiskers, Bob seized it and dumped it on the scales. Sure enough, it registered exactly 4lb. 'I told you,' he said, 'there's our steak — but where's the bloody cat?'

*   *   *

Moira, a bonny 18-year-old, asked her father: 'Dad, will it be all right to go to Oban with my boy-friend for the weekend?'

'I don't know,' said her father, 'with your mother visiting your Aunt Lizzy in Dunfermline . . .'

'Come on, Dad,' she wheedled, 'don't be so old-fashioned.'

'I'll tell you what, lass, just as long as you promise not to let him come into your room. You know how your mother worries.'

When she came back, her father's first question was: 'Now, did you keep your promise?'

'Aye, I did,' said Moira. 'I just went to his room – let *his* mother worry.'

*   *   *

A creditor in London wrote to a firm in Aberdeen, demanding immediate payment of a long overdue account. They received this reply:
'Please note that at the end of every month we place all unpaid accounts in a large pile on the table. Out of these, we draw six and pay them. Any more impudence from you and you won't get into the draw at all!'

*　　*　　*

'Hey, Jimmy, ish thish Alcoholicks Anonymush?'
'It is, indeed. Do you wish to join?'
'Naw – tae resign!'

*　　*　　*

The old couple had gone into an Inverness restaurant and ordered chops. The waiter noticed the woman hadn't touched hers and asked if they were to her liking.
'Oh, aye,' she replied. 'Ah'm just waiting for Sandy tae finish. He's using the teeth first.'

*　　*　　*

Bob, an inveterate poacher, was to appear in court yet again, so his worried friends decided to hire a very able young lawyer.

He very convincingly proved his client's innocence – claiming he hadn't been within 15 miles of the river.

Case dismissed. Then up speaks Bob:
'Does that mean ah can keep the fish?'

*   *   *

An English tourist, trying to take the mickey out of a ploughman, pointed to a scarecrow and sneered: 'One of the natives, I suppose?'

'Naw, naw,' came the reply. 'Just a summer visitor.'

*   *   *

'That shower will fairly bring things out of the ground,' said one farmer to another.

'God forbid,' came the reply. 'I've three wives there!'

*   *   *

A Scot went to see a psychiatrist. 'Tell me,' said the head-shrinker, leading him to the couch, 'when did you first start to enjoy standing a round?'

*　　*　　*

The local newspaper sent a young lad to photograph the village worthy, who was 98. When he had done so, he said to the old Scot: 'I hope I'll be back to take your picture when you reach 100.'
'Ah don't see why not,' retorted the man, 'you look healthy enough tae me!'

*　　*　　*

Archie visited his doctor complaining of seeing striped haggis when he tried to get to sleep.
'Have you ever seen a psychiatrist?' asked the doctor.
'Naw,' replied Archie. 'Jist striped haggis.'

*　　*　　*

Jock, all the way from Aberdeen, emigrated to America and applied for a job in the police. In the course of his examination, he was asked: 'What would you do to disperse a crowd?'
Replied Jock: 'Do what I'd do at home – pass round the hat!'

*　　*　　*

The branch line between Leuchars and St Andrews was noted for being very slow, which caused one traveller to say as he changed trains: 'Well, that's the worst part of my journey over.'
'Where are you off to?' asked a fellow passenger.
'Australia.'

*　　*　　*

A drunk was helped by his pal to stagger into a Temperance Hotel in the Borders.
'You can't bring him in here!' shouted the outraged proprietor.
'S'all right,' replied his pal. 'He's too far gone to notice.'

*　　*　　*

Three ex-Army pals met in a pub. The Englishman stood a round, the Irishman stood a round . . . and the Scot stood 6ft 2 in.

*   *   *

An Aberdonian, approached by a cousin for a loan of £50, said it wasn't possible because 'all my available funds are tied up in cash.'

*   *   *

The Scots angler died, made his way to heaven, and was stopped at the gate by St Peter, who said: 'You've told too many lies to get in here,'
'Have a heart,' replied the angler, 'remember you were a fisherman once yourself.'

*   *   *

An Englishman, lecturing on his travels, was speaking disparagingly about the Scots in Canada and the mixing of the race with the Indians.

'You'll find,' he said, 'a great number of Scots half-breeds and French half-breeds, but you cannot find any English half-breeds.'

'Not surprisingly,' shouted a Scot in the audience. 'The squaws had to draw the line somewhere.'

*　　*　　*

Mrs MacPherson was complaining about rats in the 18th floor of her multi-storey flat, so a housing official went along to investigate.

'Keep your eye on that wee hole in the skirting board,' she said. Five minutes later, a brown trout poked its nose through the hole.

'Gosh, woman,' said the astonished man, 'did you see that fish?'

'Just keep your eyes open for the rats,' replied the woman. 'We'll talk about the rising damp later.'

*　　*　　*

'What sort of whisky's this?' asked Jock.
'It's all I've got,' said the barman. 'It's McGonogle brand.'
'Jings,' said Jock, knocking it back, 'I'll be glad when ah've had enough.'

*   *   *

Who said Scots were lacking in emotion? Four were playing an exciting game of poker one night in a commercial hotel, when one dropped dead of a heart attack. The others finished the hand standing up.

*   *   *

The Texan oil millionaire fell into the burn on a Scottish golf course and was rescued by Willie, his caddy.
The grateful American asked him what favour he would like. Willie thought for a while, then asked if he could have one or two decent clubs.
So the Texan bought him Wentworth and Carnoustie.

*   *   *

Home Office researchers have at last
determined what Scotsmen do with old
razor blades. They shave with them. –
Ronnie Barker.

*   *   *

After an old Scot died, one of the
neighbours came to pay her respects.
'My, it's terrible,' she cried, 'and he
looks that happy.'
'Aye,' said his widow, 'Charlie was
always a bit slow on the uptake.'

*   *   *

After a taxi was involved in an accident
in Aberdeen, the local paper reported
that two passengers were detained in
hospital and the other nine allowed
home.

*   *   *

Then there was the Scots bride who kept
the bouquet and threw the groom away.

*   *   *

A Dundee shopkeeper packed his window with bagpipes and shotguns. 'Does it sell merchandise?' asked a friend.

'Sure does,' replied the shopkeeper. 'One day someone comes in tae buy bagpipes. Twa days later, his neighbours buy shotguns.'

* * *

McGregor, a big business tycoon, always kept a bowl of goldfish on his desk. When a friend asked him why, he replied: 'I just like to have something around here that opens its mouth without askin' fur a rise.'

* * *

'Has anybody offered you a meal in exchange for a good day's work?' a woman asked a tramp in a Dundee street.

'Aye, once,' replied the tramp. 'Apart fae that, ah've been shown nothin' but kindness.'

* * *

I could tell it was a Scottish restaurant –
there were forks in the sugar bowl. – Les
Dawson.

* * *

Every night Jock would go into the same
pub and order two whiskies – one for his
pal Jimmy, who had passed on.
One evening, he went into the pub and
asked for only one whisky.
'What's the matter?' asked the barman.
'You always ask for two.'
'Aye,' explained Jock, 'but I've stopped
drinking.'

* * *

'My father asks if he can borrow your
corkscrew.'
'Aye, son, I'll bring it over myself.'

* * *

Did you hear about the Scot who asked
for a no-claims bonus on his life
insurance policy?

* * *

Under the words 'Jesus Saves' at
Glasgow Central Station someone
scrawled 'with the Woolwich'.

* * *

Mrs MacPherson asked her butcher for
a pound of haggis. 'I want tae spend the
night wi' Burns,' she said.
'Ah've nae haggis,' said the butcher.
'Here's a black pudding. Spend it wi'
Sammy Davis, Jnr.'

* * *

Angus was staggering home after a night
with his fishing pals when he came upon
a scarecrow, arms outstretched. 'Hey,
Jimmy,' he said, 'I refushe tae believe
you. There never was a trout that size.'

* * *

Did you hear about the Scotsman who
died of a heart attack after throwing a
penny to some carol singers? The string
broke.

* * *

Then there was the Ayrshire farmer who gave his chickens a bottle of whisky every day. He hoped they would start to lay Scotch eggs.

*　　*　　*

I'm like an Aberdonian when it comes to money. I hate to part with it once I've memorised the serial numbers. – Jack Benny.

*　　*　　*

'Rooms overlooking the sea are £2 a day extra,' said the hotel manager.
'How much,' asked Angus, 'if ah promise not tae look?'

*　　*　　*

A number of Scottish soldiers were court-martialled for wrecking a public-house, and one of them was asked to explain to the court how the trouble had started.

'Well, sir,' he said, 'Private McSporran called Private McDougall a liar, and Private Paterson hit him over the head with a chair. Private Fraser pulled out his dirk and cut a slice out of Private McDougall's leg.

'Two or three of Private McDougall's mates piled on to Private Fraser, and a couple of others started throwing glasses and tables around. One thing led to another and then the fighting started.'

*　　*　　*

'What's the matter, Jock?' asked a fellow salesman in a restaurant. 'You usually have a big lunch, but today you only had a sandwich. Are you on a diet?'
'No,' replied Jock, 'on commission.'

*　　*　　*

Sandy was in a taxi when the brakes failed.

'Help!' said the driver in a panic. 'I can't stop!'

'Well, can ye no' at least turn aff the meter?'

*　　*　　*

Nurse: 'I think Mr MacSpadyen's regaining consciousness, doctor. He just tried to blow the froth off his medicine.'

*　　*　　*

Heard outside a Glasgow pub: 'You drive, Jimmy. You're too drunk to sing.'

*　　*　　*

At last I've discovered the reason for the amber light in traffic lights. It gives Scots drivers the chance to start their engines. – Bernard Manning.

*　　*　　*

We've just heard that Achilles Cleaning Powder have joined with Scottish Distilleries to produce a cleaner that kills 99% of all known germs – and makes the other 1% too drunk to bother. – The Two Ronnies.

*   *   *

The meanest Scot in the world? The one who broke in next door to gas himself.

*   *   *

They've just brought out the James Bond kilt for secret agents. You press a button and the sporran fires a salvo of 25-pounder shells. Only one snag – the recoil doesn't half bring tears to your eyes. – Roy Hudd.

*   *   *

The game between Celtic and Rangers
was in its 29th minute when Celtic
scored the first goal. One spectator
cheered wildly with all the Celtic fans,
though he was not wearing the colours of
either team.

Ten minutes later, Rangers equalised.
The Rangers fans went wild, and so did
the lone spectator.

The man standing next to him said:
'Just a minute, Jock – you're yelling for
both teams.'

'That's right,' said the spectator. 'I don't
care who wins.'

'Oh, an atheist, eh?' said the second
man.

*   *   *

Jock won a competition in which the first prize was a fishing holiday in the South Sea Islands.

'What a place,' he enthused on his return. 'The whole island was surrounded by man-eating sharks. Every day I put my swimming trunks on, took my rod, and waded into the sea. And there were thousands of these man-eating sharks all around me.'

'Just a minute,' interrupted a friend, 'don't tell me you went out fishing without a boat when there were man-eating sharks in the water?'

'Of course I did,' was the reply. 'They didn't bother me at all.'

'How come?'

'I've a tattoo on my chest that says "Partick Thistle for the Cup" – and not even a shark would swallow that.'

*   *   *

They say Scotsmen have no respect for age unless it's bottled.

*   *   *

'How much are the cigars?' asked the
customer.
'50p each, two for 90p.'
'I'll take one,' said the customer,
handing over 50p.
And an Aberdonian who had been
watching the transaction put 40p on the
counter and said: 'Ah'll have the other
one.'

*　　*　　*

Aberdonians are all very good singers.
They have to be – there's no lock on the
bathroom door.

*　　*　　*

News flash: Sandy MacGregor was
found not guilty today of trying to gas
his wife by throwing her into the North
Sea.

*　　*　　*

An Englishman, an American and a Scot were having drinks together, when a fly flew into each of their drinks. The Englishman removed his with a teaspoon. The American removed his with his thumb and forefinger and put it in the ash-tray. The Scot carefully removed his – and wrung it out.

*   *   *

Statistics show that one man gets knocked down by a car in Glasgow every three hours. And he's getting bloody tired of it.

*   *   *

Then there was the Aberdonian who made his own anti-freeze. He hid her winter woollies.

*   *   *

In the old days, cows used to cut the grass in Scotland. They called them lawn mooers.

*   *   *

A car park attendant at Ayr got a winter job as a cloakroom attendant. After only a week at his new job, he had dented 17 overcoats.

*   *   *

An Inverness commercial traveller went to see a psychiatrist. He was very worried, he said, because he had developed the habit of making long-distance calls to himself.
'It worries me sick, doctor,' he gulped, 'an' it's costing me a fortune.'
The psychiatrist pondered. 'Hmmm,' he said, 'have you tried reversing the charges?'

*   *   *

Heard about the rich Aberdonian and his wife who spent the evening upstairs guarding their jewellery? Thieves broke into the house and watched television.

*   *   *

Willie and Maggie MacGregor had arrived in London on their honeymoon. 'Tell me, Maggie,' asked Willie, 'd'ye ken the difference between a taxi and a bus?'

'No,' said Maggie.

'Well, then,' said Willie, 'we'll tak' a bus tae the hotel.'

*　　*　　*

'These spoons Aunt Jessie gave us as a wedding present aren't real silver,' said the bride.

'Do ye ken anything about silver?' asked the groom.

'Naw,' replied the bride, 'but ah ken a lot aboot Aunt Jessie.'

*　　*　　*

McTavish tight-fisted? Every time he takes out a coin the Queen blinks at the light.

*　　*　　*

'How much will it cost tae cure my mother-in-law?', Sandy asked the doctor.
'At least £150,' replied the doctor.
'Forget it,' said Jock. 'Ah got a much cheaper quote fae the undertaker.'

*   *   *

On the day Aberdeen played Rangers, a man turned up at the turnstile and offered 40p.
'It's 80p for admission,' said the ticket-seller.
'That's all right – ah'm an Aberdeen supporter,' said the man. 'Ah'll only be watchin' ma ain team.'

*   *   *

When Sandy MacSporran died, they gave him a wonderful funeral. It took six strong men to carry the beer.

*   *   *

Then there were the two Scots who bumped into each other after 40 years and rushed to the nearest pub to celebrate.

'It'll be magic to have a drink together after all these years,' said one.

'Aye,' said the other, 'but dinnae forget – it's your round.'

*　*　*

Sandy staggered into a sweet shop. 'Do you sell liqueur chocolates wi' rum in them?' he asked.

'Aye, we do,' said the assistant.

'Good,' said Sandy. 'Give us three pounds of middles.'

*　*　*

Did you hear about the Scot who was shipwrecked on a desert island and captured by cannibals? They tied him to a pole, stuck spears in him, and collected the blood. Then they drank the blood and went off into a wild war dance. After a week of this, the Scot protested. 'Look,' he said, 'I don't mind being tied up here and having to watch the cabaret, but stop sticking me for the drinks.'

* * *

Mrs McTavish was seated on a bus with her son and bought a single ticket. The conductor asked the boy: 'How old are you, laddie?'
'I'm four,' replied the boy.
'And when will you be five?' asked the conductor.
'When I get off this bus,' said the lad.

* * *

An Aberdonian is the only man I know that can light a cigarette in his pocket. – Colin Crompton.

* * *

You can always tell a stranger in a Glasgow pub. He puts his drink down.

* * *

Then there was the Scots footballer who got married. Getting into bed on the first night of his honeymoon, he slipped and injured his back . . . so he sent in a substitute.

* * *

Incidentally, Scotland's top international player is said to be so rich that even his football jersey has an unlisted number.

* * *

A school-teacher asked her class to compile a list of the eleven greatest living Scots. The class duly completed their list and handed them in, except for one little boy at the back.
'What's the matter, Willie?' asked the teacher. 'Can't you finish your list?'
'Not quite,' answered the lad. 'Ah just cannae decide between Derek Johnstone or Joe Jordan at centre-forward.'

* * *

Then there was the Aberdonian who tried to cross an octopus with a chicken so his family could have a leg each.

* * *

'What dae ye want to be when ye leave school, son?'
'A lollipop man, faither.'
'Why?'
'Because they dinnae start work till they're 65.'

* * *

A drunk walked into a bar in Glasgow and asked: 'Was I in here last night?'
'Yes, you were,' replied the barmaid.
'Did ah spend much money?'
'About £30.'
'Thank God – ah thought ah'd lost it!'

* * *

The manager of a Scottish football team called the centre-forward into the office. 'Bob,' he said, 'you've played so well recently that the Board have decided to give you a special bonus. We'd like you to accept this cheque for £500.'
'Thanks a lot,' said the player. 'I'm very grateful.'
'And,' added the manager, 'if you continue to play as well for the rest of the season, the Chairman has promised to sign it.'

*   *   *

MacPherson blames baked beans for all his troubles. He won a honeymoon for two in a Heinz competition and had to get married.

*   *   *

An Aberdeen stockbroker was forced by illness to take time off from his business. In the hospital, the nurse had just taken his temperature.
'What is it now, nurse?' he asked.
'102,' she replied.
'When it gets to 102½ – sell,' said the broker.

*   *   *

It was freezing cold in the Aberdeen boarding house when the couple checked in.

'Is there any chance of a fire?' asked the husband.

'No,' said the landlady, 'there's a bucket of sand in every room.'

* * *

The barman looked up casually as a pink elephant and a purple rhinoceros marched in. 'Sorry, lads,' he said, 'Angus hasn't been in this evening.'

* * *

Next week, I'll be reviewing a book that's just become a best-seller in Scotland, entitled 'Indoor Games for Flag Days.' – Ronnie Corbett.

* * *

Alexander Graham Bell invented the telephone, but he found it was useless until he invented the second telephone. This was fine until he invented the third telephone, phoned the second, and found it engaged.

*　　*　　*

When Derek Johnstone of Rangers and Prime Minister Jim Callaghan shared top billing at a dinner in Glasgow, the Premier told Johnstone: 'Pop into Downing Street any time you're in London.'
'Thanks, I will,' replied Derek. 'What number?'

*　　*　　*

To illustrate the tight security in Argentina during the World Cup, Scotland's team manager, Ally MacLeod, said: 'The other day I saw a dog lifting its leg, and the tree moved 10 yards.'

*　　*　　*

'That rain came at the righ[...] gardener Angus. 'A day of i[...] more good in a fortnight no[...] week of it would do in a m[...]

*   *   *

Just as I was leaving a Rangers social, this fellow came up to me and asked the way to the nearest hospital. 'Go in there,' I told him, 'and sing "Danny Boy".' – Andy Cameron.

*   *   *

A police patrolman stopped a car driven by a Highlander and asked him to 'blow in this bag'.
'Certainly, officer,' he replied. 'Would you like a jig or a pibroch?'
'No, no,' explained the officer. 'This bag tells whether you've had too much to drink.'
'Och, really?' retorted the Highlander. 'I'm married to one.'

*   *   *

...ing to a Glasgow man, one of the ...antages of jogging is that it gets you ...ut in the open carrying so little of value that the muggers leave you alone.

*   *   *

Then there was the Aberdonian who invented a windscreen that wouldn't hold parking tickets.

*   *   *

And how about the Inverness man who washed his sporran and couldn't do a fling with it?

*   *   *

Inspector: 'What would you do if you found a dead horse in Ardnamurchan Terrace?'
Policeman: 'Drag it into Park Place.'
Inspector: 'Why?'
Policeman: 'I cannae spell Ardnamurchan.'

*   *   *

That's McTavish all over . . . he found a box of corn cures and went out and bought himself a pair of tight shoes.

*   *   *

An inept Englishman was pacing the hallowed greens of St Andrew's, just after missing a basic three-inch putt. 'Gad, sir,' he said to his caddie, 'golf's a funny game.'
'Aye,' returned the Scotsman, 'but it's not meant tae be.'

*   *   *

And then there was the one about the Glaswegian who won a fortune on the football pools.
'But Fergus,' said his distraught wife, 'what about the begging letters?'
'Never mind, ma dear,' came the reply. 'Just keep on sending them.'

*   *   *

When Scotland beat England at
Wembley in 1977, the joyful Scots
supporters proceeded to tear the playing
area apart.

One Scot who was leaving the ground
with a suitcase was stopped by a police
inspector.

'What have you got in there?' he asked.

'Nothing much,' replied the Scot.

'Open it up,' said the inspector.

The Scot opened the case – to reveal half
a dozen patches of turf.

'What's all that?' asked the inspector.

'Well, it's like this,' explained the Scot,
'my brother-in-law's on holiday and
ah'm keeping an eye on his garden!'

*   *   *